Instructional Guides
for Literature

HOLES

A guide for the novel by Louis Sachar
Great Works Author: Jessica Case

SHELL EDUCATION

Publishing Credits

Robin Erickson, *Production Director*; Lee Aucoin, *Creative Director*;
Timothy J. Bradley, *Illustration Manager*; Emily R. Smith, M.A.Ed., *Editorial
Director*; Amber Goff, *Editorial Assistant*; Don Tran, *Production Supervisor*;
Corinne Burton, M.A.Ed., *Publisher*

Image Credits

Cover BThaiMan/Shutterstock, DeeY/Shutterstock

Standards

© 2007 Teachers of English to Speakers of Other Languages, Inc. (TESOL)
© 2007 Board of Regents of the University of Wisconsin System. World-Class Instructional Design and Assessment (WIDA).
© Copyright 2010. National Governors Association Center for Best Practices and Council of Chief State School Officers.
All rights reserved

Shell Education

5301 Oceanus Drive
Huntington Beach, CA 92649-1030
http://www.shelleducation.com

ISBN 978-1-4258-8980-7

© 2014 Shell Educational Publishing, Inc.
Printed by: **418**
Printed in: **USA** / PO#: **PO10013**

Table of Contents

How to Use This Literature Guide

Today's standards demand rigor and relevance in the reading of complex texts. The units in this series guide teachers in a rich and deep exploration of worthwhile works of literature for classroom study. The most rigorous instruction can also be interesting and engaging!

Many current strategies for effective literacy instruction have been incorporated into these instructional guides for literature. Throughout the units, text-dependent questions are used to determine comprehension of the book as well as student interpretation of the vocabulary words. The books chosen for the series are complex exemplars of carefully crafted works of literature. Close reading is used throughout the units to guide students toward revisiting the text and using textual evidence to respond to prompts orally and in writing. Students must analyze the story elements in multiple assignments for each section of the book. All of these strategies work together to rigorously guide students through their study of literature.

The next few pages will make clear how to use this guide for a purposeful and meaningful literature study. Each section of this guide is set up in the same way to make it easier for you to implement the instruction in your classroom.

Theme Thoughts

The great works of literature used throughout this series have important themes that have been relevant to people for many years. Many of the themes will be discussed during the various sections of this instructional guide. However, it would also benefit students to have independent time to think about the key themes of the novel.

Before students begin reading, have them complete *Pre-Reading Theme Thoughts* (page 13). This graphic organizer will allow students to think about the themes outside the context of the story. They'll have the opportunity to evaluate statements based on important themes and defend their opinions. Be sure to have students keep their papers for comparison to the *Post-Reading Theme Thoughts* (page 64). This graphic organizer is similar to the pre-reading activity. However, this time, students will be answering the questions from the point of view of one of the characters of the novel. They have to think about how the character would feel about each statement and defend their thoughts. To conclude the activity, have students compare what they thought about the themes before the novel to what the characters discovered during the story.

How to Use This Literature Guide (cont.)

Vocabulary

Each teacher overview page has definitions and sentences about how key vocabulary words are used in the section. These words should be introduced and discussed with students. There are two student vocabulary activity pages in each section. On the first page, students are asked to define the words chosen by the author of this unit. On the second page in most sections, each student will select words that he or she finds interesting or difficult. For each section, choose one of these pages for your students to complete. With either assignment, you may want to have students get into pairs to discuss the meanings of the words. Allow students to use reference guides to define the words. Monitor students to make sure the definitions they have found are accurate and relate to how the words are used in the text.

On some of the vocabulary student pages, students are asked to answer text-related questions about the vocabulary words. The following question stems will help you create your own vocabulary questions if you'd like to extend the discussion.

- How does this word describe _____'s character?
- In what ways does this word relate to the problem in this story?
- How does this word help you understand the setting?
- In what ways is this word related to the story's solution?
- Describe how this word supports the novel's theme of _____.
- What visual images does this word bring to your mind?
- For what reasons might the author have chosen to use this particular word?

At times, more work with the words will help students understand their meanings. The following quick vocabulary activities are a good way to further study the words.

- Have students practice their vocabulary and writing skills by creating sentences and/or paragraphs in which multiple vocabulary words are used correctly and with evidence of understanding.
- Students can play vocabulary concentration. Students make a set of cards with the words and a separate set of cards with the definitions. Then, students lay the cards out on the table and play concentration. The goal of the game is to match vocabulary words with their definitions.
- Students can create word journal entries about the words. Students choose words they think are important and then describe why they think each word is important within the novel.

How to Use This Literature Guide (cont.)

Analyzing the Literature

After students have read each section, hold small-group or whole-class discussions. Questions are written at two levels of complexity to allow you to decide which questions best meet the needs of your students. The Level 1 questions are typically less abstract than the Level 2 questions. Level 1 is indicated by a square, while Level 2 is indicated by a triangle.

These questions focus on the various story elements, such as character, setting, and plot. Student pages are provided if you want to assign these questions for individual student work before your group discussion. Be sure to add further questions as your students discuss what they've read. For each question, a few key points are provided for your reference as you discuss the novel with students.

Reader Response

In today's classrooms, there are often great readers who are below average writers. So much time and energy is spent in classrooms getting students to read on grade level, that little time is left to focus on writing skills. To help teachers include more writing in their daily literacy instruction, each section of this guide has a literature-based reader response prompt. Each of the three genres of writing is used in the reader responses within this guide: narrative, informative/explanatory, and opinion/argument. Students have a choice between two prompts for each reader response. One response requires students to make connections between the reading and their own lives. The other prompt requires students to determine text-to-text connections or connections within the text.

Close Reading the Literature

Within each section, students are asked to closely reread a short section of text. Since some versions of the novels have different page numbers, the selections are described by chapter and location along with quotations to guide the readers. After each close reading, there are text-dependent questions to be answered by students.

Encourage students to read each question one at a time and then go back to the text and discover the answer. Work with students to ensure that they use the text to determine their answers rather than making unsupported inferences. Once students have answered the questions, discuss what they discovered. Suggested answers are provided in the answer key.

How to Use This Literature Guide (cont.)

Close Reading the Literature (cont.)

These generic, open-ended stems can be used to write your own text-dependent questions if you would like to give students more practice.

- Give evidence from the text to support . . . .
- Justify your thinking using text evidence about . . . .
- Find evidence to support your conclusions about . . . .
- What text evidence helps the reader understand . . . ?
- Use the book to tell why _____ happens.
- Based on events in the story, ...
- Use text evidence to tell why . . . .

Making Connections

The activities in this section help students make cross-curricular connections to writing, mathematics, science, social studies, or the fine arts. In some of these lessons, students are asked to use the author as a mentor. The writing in the novel models a skill for them that they can then try to emulate. Students may also be asked to look for examples of language conventions within the novel. Each of these types of activities requires higher-order thinking skills from students.

Creating with the Story Elements

It is important to spend time discussing the common story elements in literature. Understanding the characters, setting, and plot can increase students' comprehension and appreciation of the story. If teachers discuss these elements daily, students will more likely internalize the concepts and look for the elements in their independent reading. Another important reason for focusing on the story elements is that students will be better writers if they think about how the stories they read are constructed.

Students are given three options for working with the story elements. They are asked to create something related to the characters, setting, or plot of the novel. Students are given choice on this activity so that they can decide to complete the activity that most appeals to them. Different multiple intelligences are used so that the activities are diverse and interesting to all students.

How to Use This Literature Guide (cont.)

Culminating Activity

This open-ended, cross-curricular activity requires higher-order thinking and allows for a creative product. Students will enjoy getting the chance to share what they have discovered through reading the novel. Be sure to allow them enough time to complete the activity at school or home.

Comprehension Assessment

The questions in this section are modeled after current standardized tests to help students analyze what they've read and prepare for tests they may see in their classrooms. The questions are dependent on the text and require critical-thinking skills to answer.

Response to Literature

The final post-reading activity is an essay based on the text that also requires further research by students. This is a great way to extend this book into other curricular areas. A suggested rubric is provided for teacher reference.

Correlation to the Standards

Shell Education is committed to producing educational materials that are research and standards based. In this effort, we have correlated all of our products to the academic standards of all 50 United States, the District of Columbia, the Department of Defense Dependents Schools, and all Canadian provinces.

How To Find Standards Correlations

To print a customized correlation report of this product for your state, visit our website at http://www.shelleducation.com and follow the on-screen directions. If you require assistance in printing correlation reports, please contact Customer Service at 1-877-777-3450.

Purpose and Intent of Standards

Standards are designed to focus instruction and guide adoption of curricula. Standards are statements that describe the criteria necessary for students to meet specific academic goals. They define the knowledge, skills, and content students should acquire at each level. Standards are also used to develop standardized tests to evaluate students' academic progress. Teachers are required to demonstrate how their lessons meet standards. Standards are used in the development of all of our products, so educators can be assured they meet high academic standards.

Correlation to the Standards (cont.)

Standards Correlation Chart

The lessons in this guide were written to support the Common Core College and Career Readiness Anchor Standards. This chart indicates which sections of this guide address the anchor standards.

Common Core College and Career Readiness Anchor Standard	Section
CCSS.ELA-Literacy.CCRA.R.1—Read closely to determine what the text says explicitly and to make logical inferences from it; cite specific textual evidence when writing or speaking to support conclusions drawn from the text.	Close Reading the Literature Sections 1–5; Making Connections Sections 2, 4; Creating with the Story Elements Sections 1–5; Culminating Activity
CCSS.ELA-Literacy.CCRA.R.2—Determine central ideas or themes of a text and analyze their development; summarize the key supporting details and ideas.	Analyzing the Literature Sections 1–5; Creating with the Story Elements Section 5; Post-Reading Response to Literature
CCSS.ELA-Literacy.CCRA.R.3—Analyze how and why individuals, events, or ideas develop and interact over the course of a text.	Analyzing the Literature Sections 1–5; Creating with the Story Elements Sections 2–3, 5
CCSS.ELA-Literacy.CCRA.R.4—Interpret words and phrases as they are used in a text, including determining technical, connotative, and figurative meanings, and analyze how specific word choices shape meaning or tone.	Vocabulary Sections 1–5; Making Connections Section 1; Culminating Activity
CCSS.ELA-Literacy.CCRA.R.10—Read and comprehend complex literary and informational texts independently and proficiently.	Entire Unit
CCSS.ELA-Literacy.CCRA.W.1—Write arguments to support claims in an analysis of substantive topics or texts using valid reasoning and relevant and sufficient evidence.	Reader Response Sections 1–3; Post-Reading Response to Literature
CCSS.ELA-Literacy.CCRA.W.2—Write informative/explanatory texts to examine and convey complex ideas and information clearly and accurately through the effective selection, organization, and analysis of content.	Reader Response Sections 1, 4–5; Making Connections Section 1
CCSS.ELA-Literacy.CCRA.W.3—Write narratives to develop real or imagined experiences or events using effective technique, well-chosen details and well-structured event sequences.	Reader Response Sections 2–5; Making Connections Section 3

Correlation to the Standards (cont.)

Standards Correlation Chart (cont.)

Common Core College and Career Readiness Anchor Standard	Section
CCSS.ELA-Literacy.CCRA.W.4—Produce clear and coherent writing in which the development, organization, and style are appropriate to task, purpose, and audience.	Making Connections Sections 3–4; Post-Reading Response to Literature
CCSS.ELA-Literacy.CCRA.L.1—Demonstrate command of the conventions of standard English grammar and usage when writing or speaking.	Analyzing the Literature Sections 1–5; Making Connections Sections 3–4
CCSS.ELA-Literacy.CCRA.L.4—Determine or clarify the meaning of unknown and multiple-meaning words and phrases by using context clues, analyzing meaningful word parts, and consulting general and specialized reference materials, as appropriate.	Vocabulary Sections 1–5
CCSS.ELA-Literacy.CCRA.L.6—Acquire and use accurately a range of general academic and domain-specific words and phrases sufficient for reading, writing, speaking, and listening at the college and career readiness level; demonstrate independence in gathering vocabulary knowledge when encountering an unknown term important to comprehension or expression.	Vocabulary Sections 1–5

TESOL and WIDA Standards

The lessons in this book promote English language development for English language learners. The following TESOL and WIDA English Language Development Standards are addressed through the activities in this book:

- **Standard 1:** English language learners communicate for social and instructional purposes within the school setting.

- **Standard 2:** English language learners communicate information, ideas and concepts necessary for academic success in the content area of language arts.

About the Author—Louis Sachar

Louis Sachar was born in New York in 1954. He lived in New York until third grade when he and his family moved to California. He was a good student but didn't really have an interest in reading until he was in high school. After high school, he attended Antioch College in Ohio but returned to California abruptly after his father passed away during the first part of his freshman year. After being home a short time, he returned to college in Berkeley, California, where he majored in economics.

While walking on campus one day, he took a flyer from a young girl who was looking for student aides to help out in her elementary school. He signed up and worked in classrooms as well as supervising recess.

After he graduated from college in 1976, he decided to use his life-changing experience at the elementary school to write a children's book, which is called *Sideways Stories From Wayside School*. An interesting fact from that story is that he used kids he knew from the elementary school in the first book. It took nine months to write his first book.

While he was writing, he decided to attend law school. He went to school at Hastings College of the Law in San Francisco. After finishing law school in 1980, he passed the bar exam and began working part-time doing legal work while also writing. He was able to quit practicing law once his books really began selling in 1989. Since that time he has been able to devote all his time to doing what he loves, writing books.

He met his wife, Carla, who was a counselor at an elementary school, while visiting there one day. She was the inspiration for the counselor character in his book, *There's a Boy in the Girl's Bathroom*. They married in 1985 and have one daughter.

Louis Sachar writes every morning but will not talk about a book he's writing until he's finished it. His wife and daughter are usually the first ones to read his new stories.

Possible Texts for Text Comparisons

There is a follow-up book to *Holes* called *Small Steps*. It follows former Camp Green Lake camper Armpit. At 17, he struggles with the challenges of being an African American teenager who has a criminal past.

Book Summary of *Holes*

Stanley Yelnats is just another regular kid whose family has a history of bad luck. His bad luck continues when he is held responsible for a crime he didn't commit. Along the way, we learn about a curse that has held his family hostage for several generations.

His bad luck lands him in a very strange correctional camp in the middle of the Texas desert. The warden has all the campers digging holes in a dry lakebed, for what reason the boys do not know.

The novel joins interesting tall tales from local history and Stanley's family history as well. The relationships among the boys in the camp are interesting and grow more complicated as the story progresses. Eventually Stanley finds a good friend, treasure, and answers about the curse on his family. He ultimately learns to like himself for who he is.

Cross-Curricular Connection

This book can be used during a social studies unit on child labor.

Possible Texts for Text Sets

- Curtis, Christopher Paul. *The Watsons Go to Birmingham—1963*. Dell Laurel Leaf, 2000.
- Fleischman, Paul. *Whirligig*. New York, 1998.
- Lowry, Lois. *The Giver*. New York, 1993.
- Paulsen, Gary. *The Car*. Harcourt, 2006.
- Peck, Richard. *A Long Way from Chicago*. 2008.

Name _____

Date _____

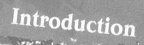

Pre-Reading Theme Thoughts

Directions: Read each of the statements in the first column. Decide if you agree or disagree with the statements. Record your opinion by marking an X in Agree or Disagree for each statement. Explain your choices in the third column. There are no right or wrong answers.

Statement	Agree	Disagree	Explain Your Answer
Fate controls what will happen in your life.			
The most important people in life are your friends.			
People sometimes take advantage of the power that is given to them.			
The lives of your ancestors affect you today.			

Vocabulary Overview

Ten key words from this section are provided below with definitions and sentences about how the words are used in the book. Choose one of the vocabulary activity sheets (pages 15 or 16) for students to complete as they read this section. Monitor the students as they work to ensure the definitions they have found are accurate and relate to the text. Finally, discuss these important vocabulary words with the students. If you think these words or other words in the section warrant more time devoted to them, there are suggestions in the introduction for other vocabulary activities (page 5).

Word	Definition	Sentence About Text
perseverance (ch. 3)	not giving up; the effort required to do something and keep doing it until the end, even if it's hard	Stanley's father shows **perseverance** by working very hard on his various projects.
deftly (ch. 7)	accomplished with style and skill	Zero **deftly** digs his hole so his shovel fits down and around the inside of the hole.
desolate (ch. 4)	a deserted, empty, depressing place	Camp Green Lake is not at all as Stanley had imagined; it is barren and **desolate**.
expanse (ch. 7)	a wide and open space or area of surface or land	A vast **expanse** of desert stretches ahead.
excavated (ch. 7)	removed or found by digging	Stanley **excavates** as much dirt as he can from his hole.
grimaced (ch. 7)	made a facial expression suggesting disgust or pain	Stanley **grimaces** as he looks down at his callused and blistered hands.
stifling (ch. 7)	characterized by oppressive heat and humidity causing difficulty breathing	The hot air is **stifling** as Stanley steps off the bus at Camp Green Lake.
preposterous (ch. 7)	absolutely absurd	Myra's father thinks it is **preposterous** that she can pick out the best pig.
forlorn (ch. 7)	showing hopelessness	Elya is so **forlorn** that Madam Zeroni decides to help him anyway.
spigot (ch. 5)	a plug for stopping the flow of a liquid	The water **spigot** on the back of the truck is a sign of relief to the very thirsty Stanley.

Name _____

Date _____

Understanding Vocabulary Words

Directions: The following words are in this section of the book. Use context clues and reference materials to determine an accurate definition for each word.

Word	Definition
perseverance (ch. 3)	
deftly (ch. 7)	
desolate (ch. 4)	
expanse (ch. 7)	
excavated (ch. 7)	
grimaced (ch. 7)	
stifling (ch. 7)	
preposterous (ch. 7)	
forlorn (ch. 7)	
spigot (ch. 5)	

Name _____

Date _____

During-Reading Vocabulary Activity

Directions: As you read these chapters, record at least eight important words on the lines below. Try to find interesting, difficult, intriguing, special, or funny words. Your words can be long or short. They can be hard or easy to spell. After each word, use context clues in the text and reference materials to define the word.

- _____
- _____
- _____
- _____
- _____
- _____
- _____
- _____
- _____
- _____

Directions: Respond to these questions about the words in this section.

1. How does the word **perseverance** describe Stanley and his family?

_____

_____

2. In what ways does Camp Green Lake seem **desolate**?

_____

_____

Analyzing the Literature

Provided below are discussion questions you can use in small groups, with the whole class, or for written assignments. Each question is given at two levels so you can choose the right question for each group of students. Activity sheets with these questions are provided (pages 18–19) if you want students to write their responses. For each question, a few key discussion points are provided for your reference.

Story Element	■ Level 1	▲ Level 2	Key Discussion Points
Character	Describe Stanley both before going to camp and while in camp.	Compare and contrast Stanley to the rest of his family.	When discussing Stanley, students need to mention his and his family's struggle to have any kind of good luck. Characterization of Stanley and his family are pivotal to the understanding of their past and Stanley's role in this book.
Setting	In what ways is Camp Green Lake similar to and different from traditional camps?	Which aspects of the setting at Camp Green Lake seem possible and which seem impossible?	Camp Green Lake is different from other normal camp settings. The boys don't have free time to play or do outdoor adventures. There are guards instead of counselors. It may seem impossible to students that a camp like this could exist.
Character	Who is Zero, and why is he important?	In what ways will Zero play an important role in this story?	Zero adds some interest and curiosity to the plot. He gives the reader a perspective of Camp Green Lake other than the view given by Stanley. Their relationship is a pivotal part of this storyline.
Plot	What is the problem in this story?	Describe how the problem in the story may relate to Stanley's family's past.	Within the first section of this book the overarching problem begins to show itself. The holes the boys are digging have something to do with Stanley's family, but the connection is not very strong at this point.

Name _____

Date _____

Analyzing the Literature

Directions: Think about the section you have just read. Read each question and state your response with textual evidence.

1. Describe Stanley both before going to camp and while in camp.

   _____

   _____

   _____

   _____

2. In what ways is Camp Green Lake similar to and different from traditional camps?

   _____

   _____

   _____

   _____

3. Who is Zero, and why is he important?

   _____

   _____

   _____

   _____

4. What is the problem in this story?

   _____

   _____

   _____

   _____

Name _____

Date _____

▲ Analyzing the Literature

Directions: Think about the section you have just read. Read each question and state your response with textual evidence.

1. Compare and contrast Stanley to the rest of his family.

   _____

   _____

   _____

   _____

2. Which aspects of the setting at Camp Green Lake seem possible and which seem impossible?

   _____

   _____

   _____

   _____

3. In what ways will Zero play an important role in this story?

   _____

   _____

   _____

   _____

4. Describe how the problem in the story may relate to Stanley's family's past.

   _____

   _____

   _____

   _____

Name _____

Date _____

Reader Response

Directions: Choose one of the following prompts about this section to answer. Be sure you include a topic sentence in your response, use textual evidence to support your opinion, and provide a strong conclusion that summarizes your opinion.

Writing Prompts

- **Informative/Explanatory Piece**—In this section, you meet Stanley Yelnats. Explain why you would or would not like to have him as a friend.
- **Opinion/Argument Piece**—What are the most important details that Louis Sachar includes to make the story realistic?

_____

_____

_____

_____

_____

_____

_____

_____

_____

_____

_____

_____

_____

Name _____

Date _____

Close Reading the Literature

Directions: Closely reread the section where readers finally find out why Stanley is sent to Camp Green Lake. Start toward the beginning of chapter 6 where it states, "Now, as Stanley lay on his cot, . . ." Continue reading until the end of the chapter. Read each question and then revisit the text to find the evidence that supports your answer.

1. What text evidence helps the reader understand the judge's decision to send Stanley to Camp Green Lake?

   _____

   _____

   _____

2. Give evidence from the text to describe the Stanley Yelnats that the judge gets to know.

   _____

   _____

   _____

3. Use the book to tell how Stanley feels about the judge's decision to send him to Camp Green Lake.

   _____

   _____

   _____

4. Based on this scene what effect do you think the judge's decision will have on Stanley's life?

   _____

   _____

   _____

   _____

Name _____

Date _____

Making Connections–Homelessness

Directions: Stanley's friend was homeless before he came to camp. Discuss with a few other students homelessness in your community or in communities near you. What would it be like to be homeless? Create a poster advocating a way that people can help end this societal problem.

Creating with the Story Elements

Directions: Thinking about the story elements of character, setting, and plot in a novel is very important to understanding what is happening and why. Complete **one** of the following activities about what you've read so far. Be creative and have fun!

Characters

Draw a picture of Stanley as he digs his first hole at Camp Green Lake. In your picture, include details for the character as well as details about the hole he is digging.

Setting

Create a brochure advertising Camp Green Lake. The brochure should give at least four reasons why people might want to visit, include a map, accommodations, and attractions.

Plot

Recreate this cause-and-effect flow chart with predictions. To do this, write an event in a box, list what causes it and what effect it has. Then make a prediction as to what might happen next.

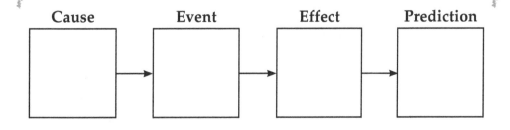

Cause	Event	Effect	Prediction

Vocabulary Overview

Ten key words from this section are provided below with definitions and sentences about how the words are used in the book. Choose one of the vocabulary activity sheets (pages 25 or 26) for students to complete as they read this section. Monitor the students as they work to ensure the definitions they have found are accurate and relate to the text. Finally, discuss these important vocabulary words with the students. If you think these words or other words in the section warrant more time devoted to them, there are suggestions in the introduction for other vocabulary activities (page 5).

Word	Definition	Sentence about Text
predatory (ch. 8)	animals that kill and then eat or "prey on" other animals	A hole is a great place for a yellow-spotted lizard to live so he can hide from the **predatory** birds.
upholstery (ch. 9)	the covering on furniture	The **upholstery** on the chairs in the recreation room looks worn.
stationery (ch. 9)	a set of writing paper	Stanley takes his pen and **stationery** to the recreation room.
scowled (ch. 9)	made an angry face	Stanley is **scowled** at by Squid for writing a note to his mother.
radiated (ch. 10)	sent out waves or rays of light	The sun **radiates** over the boys as they dig their holes.
engraved (ch. 13)	cut or impressed into a surface	The tube Stanley finds has a design **engraved** on it.
paranoid (ch. 15)	someone who has an irrational and obsessive distrust of others	Zigzag seems **paranoid** as he tells Stanley how the warden watches them all the time.
presumably (ch. 15)	indicates a logical conclusion for which you don't have definite proof	The warden tells the boys to dig in the hole where the tube was **presumably** found.
appropriate (ch. 15)	when something is suitable or fitting for a situation	It is **appropriate** for the boys to dig in the hole after the tube is found in it.
evict (ch. 16)	expel or eject from a location	Stanley's father's new invention might get them **evicted** from their home.

Name _____

Date _____

Understanding Vocabulary Words

Directions: The following words are in this section of the book. Use context clues and reference materials to determine an accurate definition for each word.

Word	Definition
predatory (ch. 8)	
upholstery (ch. 9)	
stationery (ch. 9)	
scowled (ch. 9)	
radiated (ch. 10)	
engraved (ch. 13)	
paranoid (ch. 15)	
presumably (ch. 15)	
appropriate (ch. 15)	
evict (ch. 16)	

Name _____

Date _____

During-Reading Vocabulary Activity

Directions: As you read these chapters, record at least eight important words on the lines below. Try to find interesting, difficult, intriguing, special, or funny words. Your words can be long or short. They can be hard or easy to spell. After each word, use context clues in the text and reference materials to define the word.

- _____
- _____
- _____
- _____
- _____
- _____
- _____
- _____
- _____
- _____

Directions: Respond to these questions about the words in this section.

1. How does the **engraved** design found on the bottom of the tube relate to the plot?

   _____

   _____

2. How has X-Ray started to become **paranoid** about the warden watching them?

   _____

   _____

Analyzing the Literature

Provided below are discussion questions you can use in small groups, with the whole class, or for written assignments. Each question is given at two levels so you can choose the right question for each group of students. Activity sheets with these questions are provided (pages 28–29) if you want students to write their responses. For each question, a few key discussion points are provided for your reference.

Story Element	■ Level 1	▲ Level 2	Key Discussion Points
Character	Describe how X-Ray plays an important role in this section of the book.	Describe the relationship, as it now stands, between Stanley and X-Ray.	X-Ray shows himself as the leader of the group by his interactions with the other boys. Stanley starts to respect X-Ray by giving him the tube, and in return X-Ray allows him to move ahead of somebody else in the water line. The evolution of X-Ray brings out a different side of Stanley.
Plot	What is the problem in the story now?	Describe how the problem now is different from what it was in chapters 1–7.	The plot has now become more involved and is starting to show a connection to Stanley's family's past. The tube Stanley found is greatly significant to why the boys are digging holes.
Setting	Describe the boys' recreation room.	Is it ironic that the boys have trashed their recreation room? Why or why not?	The boys treat the recreation room as they might their own room at home. They don't take care of the place because that place does not hold great memories for them.
Conflict	Why does Stanley not want to give the tube to X-Ray?	In what ways will Stanley finding the tube help him or hurt him in this story?	Stanley deals with a great deal of internal conflict in this section. He struggles between what is perceived as right (giving the tube to X-Ray) and his own needs. He must make a decision that might not end up in his favor.

Name _____

Date _____

Analyzing the Literature

Directions: Think about the section you have just read. Read each question and state your response with textual evidence.

1. Describe how X-Ray plays an important role in this section of the book.

_____

_____

_____

_____

2. What is the problem in the story now?

_____

_____

_____

_____

3. Describe the boys' recreation room.

_____

_____

_____

_____

4. Why does Stanley not want to give the tube to X-Ray?

_____

_____

_____

_____

Name _____

Date _____

▲ Analyzing the Literature

Directions: Think about the section you have just read. Read each question and state your response with textual evidence.

1. Describe the relationship, as it now stands, between Stanley and X-Ray.

_____

_____

_____

_____

2. Describe how the problem now is different from what it was in chapters 1–7.

_____

_____

_____

_____

3. Is it ironic that the boys have trashed their recreation room? Why or why not?

_____

_____

_____

_____

4. In what ways will Stanley finding the tube help him or hurt him in this story?

_____

_____

_____

_____

Name _____

Date _____

Reader Response

Directions: Choose one of the following prompts about this section to answer. Be sure you include a topic sentence in your response, use textual evidence to support your opinion, and provide a strong conclusion that summarizes your opinion.

Writing Prompts

- **Narrative Piece**—Tell about a few real-life people or events that you are reminded of by the characters and events in the story.
- **Opinion/Argument Piece**—Explore how Stanley is changing throughout this story. Describe what you think is the most important change he has experienced.

_____

_____

_____

_____

_____

_____

_____

_____

_____

_____

_____

_____

_____

_____

_____

_____

Name _____

Date _____

Close Reading the Literature

Directions: Closely reread the following section in chapter 13. Start reading at the beginning of the chapter and stop reading when Zigzag asks Stanley what he has. Read each question and then revisit the text to find the evidence that supports your answer.

1. Use the text to tell why Stanley is hesitant to give the tube he finds to X-Ray.

   _____

   _____

   _____

   _____

2. What text evidence helps the reader understand how Stanley feels as he finds the tube?

   _____

   _____

   _____

   _____

3. In what ways is it becoming easier for Stanley to dig the holes at Camp Green Lake?

   _____

   _____

   _____

   _____

4. Based on the events in the story up to this point, why do you think the engraved design looks familiar to Stanley?

   _____

   _____

   _____

   _____

Name _____

Date _____

Making Connections–A Desert Habitat

Directions: The setting of this story takes place in an extremely large, dry desert known to the campers as Camp Green Lake. Create either a diorama or a three-dimensional model of how you imagine Camp Green Lake looks. Don't forget to include the Warden's place, the compound, and tents where the boys spend their down time. Use the space below to brainstorm ideas for your creation.

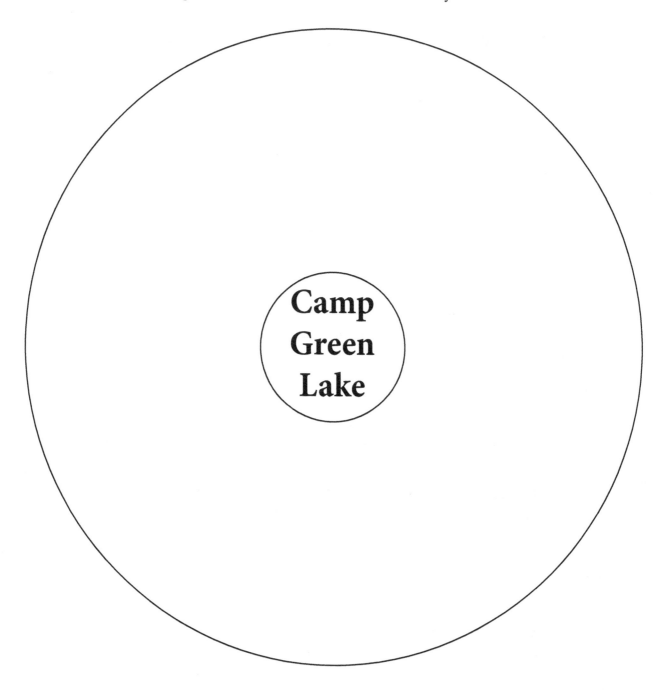

Camp Green Lake

Name _____

Date _____

Creating with the Story Elements

Directions: Thinking about the story elements of character, setting, and plot in a novel is very important to understanding what is happening and why. Complete **one** of the following activities about what you've read so far. Be creative and have fun!

Characters

Recreate the following graphic organizer to show what you have learned about X-Ray in this section. List descriptive words that capture his personality, and then provide direct evidence from the text that shows how he acts and looks.

Descriptive Words	Evidence

Setting

Draw a picture of the recreation room (or Wreck Room). In your picture, be sure to include labels and details about the room using evidence from the novel.

Plot

If you take X-Ray out of the story, Stanley would have been able to show Mr. Pendanski the tube he finds. How might this have changed the plot of the story? Recreate this pivotal scene in your own creative way to show how the plot would have changed without X-Ray. You can create a comic strip, write it as a poem, draw it into a graphic novel, etc. Be creative!

Vocabulary Overview

Ten key words from this section are provided below with definitions and sentences about how the words are used in the book. Choose one of the vocabulary activity sheets (pages 35 or 36) for students to complete as they read this section. Monitor the students as they work to ensure the definitions they have found are accurate and relate to the text. Finally, discuss these important vocabulary words with the students. If you think these words or other words in the section warrant more time devoted to them, there are suggestions in the introduction for other vocabulary activities (page 5).

Word	Definition	Sentence About Text
calloused (ch. 18)	skin that is thickened and rough from rubbing against something	Stanley's hands have become **calloused** from using the shovel day after day.
defiance (ch. 22)	when someone or a group openly challenges authority	Magnet's **defiance** lands Stanley in the Warden's cabin.
concoctions (ch. 25)	curious mixtures of things like a bunch of liquids	The Warden has a **concoction** of nail polish and rattlesnake venom in a bottle.
refuge (ch. 21)	to find a safe place	Stanley's great-grandfather takes **refuge** on a rock after Kissin' Kate Barlow robs him in the desert.
recede (ch. 20)	to pull back, retreat, or become faint or distant	Three days after the warden scratches Mr. Sir, the marks are finally starting to **recede**.
penetrating (ch. 18)	forcing into or piercing through	Trout Walker's motorized boat **penetrates** Sam's boat.
systematic (ch. 24)	something that is carefully planned	Mr. Sir is **systematic** in not giving Sam water in his canteen.
precipice (ch. 28)	the edge of a steep cliff	Kate looks out over a **precipice**.
increments (ch. 28)	small amounts	Over small **increments** of time Sam visits the schoolhouse on a daily basis.
dread (ch. 28)	the fear of something bad happening	**Dread** fills Linda Walker when Kate won't tell where she buried the loot.

Name _____

Date _____

Understanding Vocabulary Words

Directions: The following words are in this section of the book. Use context clues and reference materials to determine an accurate definition for each word.

Word	Definition
calloused (ch. 18)	
defiance (ch. 22)	
concoctions (ch. 25)	
refuge (ch. 21)	
recede (ch. 20)	
penetrating (ch. 18)	
systematic (ch. 24)	
precipice (ch. 28)	
increments (ch. 28)	
dread (ch. 28)	

Name _____

Date _____

During-Reading Vocabulary Activity

Directions: As you read these chapters, record at least eight important words on the lines below. Try to find interesting, difficult, intriguing, special, or funny words. Your words can be long or short. They can be hard or easy to spell. After each word, use context clues in the text and reference materials to define the word.

- _____

- _____

- _____

- _____

- _____

- _____

- _____

- _____

- _____

- _____

Directions: Now, organize your words. Rewrite each of your words on a sticky note. Work as a group to create a bar graph of your words. You should stack any words that are the same on top of one another. Different words appear in different columns. Finally, discuss with your teacher why certain words were chosen more often than other words.

Analyzing the Literature

Provided below are discussion questions you can use in small groups, with the whole class, or for written assignments. Each question is given at two levels so you can choose the right question for each group of students. Activity sheets with these questions are provided (pages 38–39) if you want students to write their responses. For each question, a few key discussion points are provided for your reference.

Story Element	■ Level 1	▲ Level 2	Key Discussion Points
Plot	How do the initials K.B. change the plot of this story?	How do Stanley's thoughts about the initials K.B. change the plot of this story?	Stanley notices K.B. engraved on the warden's makeup. His mother has makeup with the same initials. He makes the connection between the initials and Kate Barlow.
Character	Who is Kissin' Kate Barlow?	How does Katherine Barlow evolve into Kissin' Kate Barlow?	Kate Barlow is the only schoolteacher in Green Lake. She falls in love with Sam (an African American) and when the town finds out they kill him. She seeks revenge on the town and curses it.
Character	What do we learn about Zero's character?	How does Zero and Stanley's friendship compare and contrast to what we already knew about each of them?	Zero has never really spoken before now. He sticks up for Stanley when Stanley takes the blame for the seeds. They make a deal where Zero helps dig Stanley's hole and Stanley teaches Zero how to read.
Setting	How has the desert changed over the last 100 years?	Compare the desert at Camp Green Lake to the Green Lake that was there 100 years ago.	One hundred years ago there was actually a lake. Kate cursed the town after they killed Sam, and it has not rained there since. Kate's treasure is said to be buried on the lake, hence the reason for all the holes.

Name _____

Date _____

Analyzing the Literature

Directions: Think about the section you have just read. Read each question and state your response with textual evidence.

1. How do the initials K.B. change the plot of this story?

_____

_____

_____

_____

2. Who is Kissin' Kate Barlow?

_____

_____

_____

_____

3. What do we learn about Zero's character?

_____

_____

_____

_____

4. How has the desert changed over the last 100 years?

_____

_____

_____

_____

Name

Date

▲ Analyzing the Literature

Directions: Think about the section you have just read. Read each question and state your response with textual evidence.

1. How do Stanley's thoughts about the initials K.B. change the plot of this story?

_____

_____

_____

_____

2. How does Katherine Barlow evolve into Kissin' Kate Barlow?

_____

_____

_____

_____

3. How does Zero and Stanley's friendship compare and contrast to what we already knew about each of them?

_____

_____

_____

_____

4. Compare the desert at Camp Green Lake to the Green Lake that was there 100 years ago.

_____

_____

_____

_____

Name _____

Date _____

Reader Response

Directions: Choose one of the following prompts about this section to answer. Be sure you include a topic sentence in your response, use textual evidence to support your opinion, and provide a strong conclusion that summarizes your opinion.

Writing Prompts

- **Narrative Piece**—If you were a character in this novel, how would it affect the plot? Rewrite a scene from this section with you added to the scene.
- **Opinion/Argument Piece**—This book has three plots that are all connected. Which of the three plots do you find the most interesting: Stanley, Katherine Barlow, or Madame Zeroni? Support your choice with evidence from the story.

_____

_____

_____

_____

_____

_____

_____

_____

_____

_____

_____

_____

_____

_____

Name _____

Date _____

Close Reading the Literature

Directions: Closely reread chapter 26. Make sure to pay careful attention to the part at the end that details what happens after Sam is killed. Read each question and then revisit the text to find the evidence that supports your answer.

1. How does the sheriff react when Kate comes to him for help? Use evidence from the text to support your answer.

   _____

   _____

   _____

   _____

2. Use the book to tell how the townspeople of Green Lake feel about an African American man and a white woman kissing.

   _____

   _____

   _____

   _____

3. Give evidence from the text to describe how Sam and Kate try to escape the townspeople.

   _____

   _____

   _____

   _____

4. Based on the last scene in chapter 26, what do you infer Kate does once she leaves Green Lake?

   _____

   _____

   _____

   _____

Name _____

Date _____

Making Connections— Dear Mom . . . Notes Home

Directions: Stanley writes letters to his mom every day after coming in from digging. His notes are about things that would typically happen at a normal camp: obstacle courses, long swims, rock climbing, etc. Pretend you are in Stanley's shoes. Write a note to your mother telling her about your normal day at camp. Remember, you don't want her to get suspicious or worried about what is really going on at camp.

_____

_____

_____

_____

_____

_____

_____

_____

_____

_____

_____

_____

_____

_____

Name _____

Date _____

Creating with the Story Elements

Directions: Thinking about the story elements of character, setting, and plot in a novel is very important to understanding what is happening and why. Complete **one** of the following activities about what you've read so far. Be creative and have fun!

Characters

Create an acrostic poem about Zero. You can use either Zero or his given name, Hector. Be creative and use descriptive words.

Setting

A desert habitat is an interesting place filled with various animals and plants. Create a brochure about the desert that is Camp Green Lake. Be sure to include the following:

- weather
- history
- map
- activities

Plot

Create a visual storyboard detailing the events that have happened thus far in the story. Make sure to include at least 10 events. Just include major events that move the story forward.

Vocabulary Overview

Ten key words from this section are provided below with definitions and sentences about how the words are used in the book. Choose one of the vocabulary activity sheets (pages 45 or 46) for students to complete as they read this section. Monitor the students as they work to ensure the definitions they have found are accurate and relate to the text. Finally, discuss these important vocabulary words with the students. If you think these words or other words in the section warrant more time devoted to them, there are suggestions in the introduction for other vocabulary activities (page 5).

Word	Definition	Sentence about Text
humid (ch. 29)	when there is a lot of moisture in the air	Stanley is drenched in sweat from the **humid** weather out on the dry lake.
horizon (ch. 30)	the line where the sky meets the earth	Stanley sees the **horizon** as he looks out over the desert.
delirious (ch. 29)	when one becomes incoherent or hallucinates	Stanley's great-grandfather becomes **delirious** while stranded in the desert.
jut (ch. 30)	to extend outward	A part of the mountain that Stanley can see **juts** upward.
feeble (ch. 30)	lacking strength	Stanley feels **feeble** after digging in his hole all day in the hot sun.
riot (ch. 30)	a rowdy group of people causing problems	A **riot** ensues between Stanley and the other campers.
fidgeting (ch. 32)	making small, little movements usually with one's hands and feet	Zero is **fidgeting** while talking with the warden.
lurched (ch. 32)	suddenly moved, usually forward	When Stanley hits a hole with the truck, it **lurches** forward.
mirage (ch. 34)	an optical illusion	Stanley thinks he sees water, but it is just a **mirage**.
protruding (ch. 36)	something that is sticking out	Half of the boat is **protruding** out of the ground.

Name _____

Date _____

Understanding Vocabulary Words

Directions: The following words are in this section of the book. Use context clues and reference materials to determine an accurate definition for each word.

Word	Definition
humid (ch. 29)	
horizon (ch. 30)	
delirious (ch. 29)	
jut (ch. 30)	
feeble (ch. 30)	
riot (ch. 30)	
fidgeting (ch. 32)	
lurched (ch. 32)	
mirage (ch. 34)	
protruding (ch. 36)	

Name _____

Date _____

During-Reading Vocabulary Activity

Directions: As you read these chapters, record at least eight important words on the lines below. Try to find interesting, difficult, intriguing, special, or funny words. Your words can be long or short. They can be hard or easy to spell. After each word, use context clues in the text and reference materials to define the word.

- _____
- _____
- _____
- _____
- _____
- _____
- _____
- _____
- _____
- _____

Directions: Respond to these questions about the words in this section.

1. What events occur after Stanley's **feeble** attempt to get Zigzag to leave him alone?

   _____

   _____

2. What two ideas are significant about the **protruding** boat Stanley finds as he walks through the desert looking for Zero?

   _____

   _____

Analyzing the Literature

Provided below are discussion questions you can use in small groups, with the whole class, or for written assignments. Each question is given at two levels so you can choose the right question for each group of students. Activity sheets with these questions are provided (pages 48–49) if you want students to write their responses. For each question, a few key discussion points are provided for your reference.

Story Element	■ Level 1	▲ Level 2	Key Discussion Points
Character	What occurs to make Zero run away?	How has Zero changed since the beginning of the story?	Zero begins to trust Stanley and asks him to teach him to read. He speaks up for himself after the things Mr. Pendanski says about him. He runs away after vowing never to dig another hole.
Character	Why does Stanley go after Zero?	What has changed in Stanley since he first came to camp?	Stanley has a real friend and cares about his well being. He grows concerned for Zero after he doesn't return to camp. Stanley goes against all he has been taught at camp and leaves camp to find Zero.
Plot	How has the problem changed in this story?	Describe how the story is starting to parallel the tale of Kissin' Kate Barlow.	Stanley has made a connection as to why the warden is having them dig holes. His family is also tied to Kissin' Kate Barlow and her curse on Camp Green Lake.
Setting	What is different in this part of the desert?	How is this part of the desert different from the desert where camp is?	There are more clusters of holes that have been dug. A mountain shaped liked a big thumb is a major part of the desert. A boat is protruding from the ground.

Name _____

Date _____

Analyzing the Literature

Directions: Think about the section you have just read. Read each question and state your response with textual evidence.

1. What occurs to make Zero run away?

_____

_____

_____

_____

2. Why does Stanley go after Zero?

_____

_____

_____

_____

3. How has the problem changed in this story?

_____

_____

_____

_____

4. What is different in this part of the desert?

_____

_____

_____

_____

Name _____

Date _____

▲ Analyzing the Literature

Directions: Think about the section you have just read. Read each question and state your response with textual evidence.

1. How has Zero changed since the beginning of the story?

_____

_____

_____

_____

2. What has changed in Stanley since he first came to camp?

_____

_____

_____

_____

3. Describe how the story is starting to parallel the tale of Kissin' Kate Barlow.

_____

_____

_____

_____

4. How is this part of the desert different from the desert where camp is?

_____

_____

_____

_____

Name _____

Date _____

Reader Response

Directions: Choose one of the following prompts about this section to answer. Be sure you include a topic sentence in your response, use textual evidence to support your opinion, and provide a strong conclusion that summarizes your opinion.

Writing Prompts

- **Informative/Explanatory Piece**—Both Zero and Stanley make tough decisions in this section. When you have to make a tough decision, what steps do you take to think of options and choose the best one?
- **Narrative Piece**—Choose a short scene within this section. Rewrite the scene, changing a major aspect of it. You can change the main characters, the setting, or even the plot.

_____

_____

_____

_____

_____

_____

_____

_____

_____

_____

_____

_____

_____

_____

Name _____

Date _____

Close Reading the Literature

Directions: Closely reread the last few pages of chapter 30. Start where Stanley is explaining to the warden why Zero is digging his holes for him and continue reading to the end of the chapter. Read each question and then revisit the text to find the evidence that supports your answer.

1. What does Zero mean when he says, "I'm not digging another hole"?

   _____

   _____

   _____

   _____

2. Describe what happens to Zero after he hits Mr. Pendanski with the shovel.

   _____

   _____

   _____

   _____

3. Using evidence from the text, describe the events that lead to Zero taking off into the desert by himself.

   _____

   _____

   _____

   _____

4. Based on the events that you just read, why does the author have Stanley decide to go after Zero in the next chapter?

   _____

   _____

   _____

   _____

Name _____

Date _____

Making Connections–Cause and Effect

Directions: For the following activity you will need a set of dominoes and a partner. A series of causes and effects happen throughout chapters 29–39. Start by naming an event from this section, for example, Mr. Pendanski calls Zero stupid. Place a domino on the ground in the upright position. With your partner, take turns coming up with the different causes and effects of this event. For each, place a domino in line. Continue to line the dominoes upright one after the other as you name the chain of causes, events, and effects that occur in the story. After you have named all the major events that occur within this section of the book, knock down the first domino and watch the chain reaction in motion. Then discuss the following questions with your partner before writing your responses.

1. Describe how the dominoes relate to the events in the story.

_____

_____

_____

_____

_____

2. What events can you infer will occur as you continue reading?

_____

_____

_____

_____

_____

Extension: If you want to play again, go back to an earlier section of the book and recreate another set of events (causes and effects) that lead to a long reaction.

Name _____

Date _____

Creating with the Story Elements

Directions: Thinking about the story elements of character, setting, and plot in a novel is very important to understanding what is happening and why. Complete **one** of the following activities about what you've read so far. Be creative and have fun!

Characters

At the beginning of chapter 35 there is a great description of how Zero looks after being out in the desert alone for four days. Create a caricature of Zero as he is described in the beginning of this chapter.

Setting

In this section, we are introduced to God's Thumb and how it is connected to the camp, Stanley's great-grandfather, and Kate Barlow. Use clay to create God's Thumb as it is described.

Plot

If you were to take Stanley and Zero out of this story and place them in the middle of a fun camp, how might the confrontation with the other boys in their group have been different? Create a comic strip to show the conversations between them.

Vocabulary Overview

Ten key words from this section are provided below with definitions and sentences about how the words are used in the book. Choose one of the vocabulary activity sheets (pages 55 or 56) for students to complete as they read this section. Monitor the students as they work to ensure the definitions they have found are accurate and relate to the text. Finally, discuss these important vocabulary words with the students. If you think these words or other words in the section warrant more time devoted to them, there are suggestions in the introduction for other vocabulary activities (page 5).

Word	Definition	Sentence about Text
contritely (ch. 40)	to feel regret, remorse or even guilt	"I took the shoes," Zero said **contritely**.
inexplicable (ch. 43)	something that can't be explained	It is **inexplicable** to Stanley how he carried Zero all the way up the steep mountainside.
distinctive (ch. 43)	things that set something apart from others	The onions on Big Thumb have a **distinctive** odor.
authenticated (ch. 47)	something that is real or genuine and not counterfeit	Clyde Livingston **authenticated** the shoes Zero stole.
commotion (ch. 47)	a noisy disturbance	There was a big **commotion** when the store realized the famous shoes were gone.
precarious (ch. 47)	when something is unstable, dangerous or difficult and likely to get worse	The trip back down the mountain is a **precarious** one.
jurisdiction (ch. 48)	having legal right over something	The warden no longer has **jurisdiction** over Stanley.
pursuant (ch. 48)	something's in accordance with a particular law, ruling or request	Stanley's release papers are **pursuant** with what his lawyer says.
legitimate (ch. 48)	something is the real deal, according to the law	There is **legitimate** hope when Zero is able to go with Stanley.
delirium (ch. 47)	a mental state in which one is confused and unable to think or speak clearly	The warden experiences **delirium** as she watches the treasure leave with Stanley.

Name _____

Date _____

Understanding Vocabulary Words

Directions: The following words are in this section of the book. Use context clues and reference materials to determine an accurate definition for each word.

Word	Definition
contritely (ch. 40)	
inexplicable (ch. 43)	
distinctive (ch. 43)	
authenticated (ch. 47)	
commotion (ch. 47)	
precarious (ch. 47)	
jurisdiction (ch. 48)	
pursuant (ch. 48)	
legitimate (ch. 48)	
delirium (ch. 47)	

Name _____

Date _____

During-Reading Vocabulary Activity

Directions: As you read these chapters, choose five important words from the story. Use these words to complete the word flow chart below. On each arrow, write a word. In each box, explain how the connected pair of words relates to each other. An example for the words *jurisdiction* and *pursuant* has been done for you.

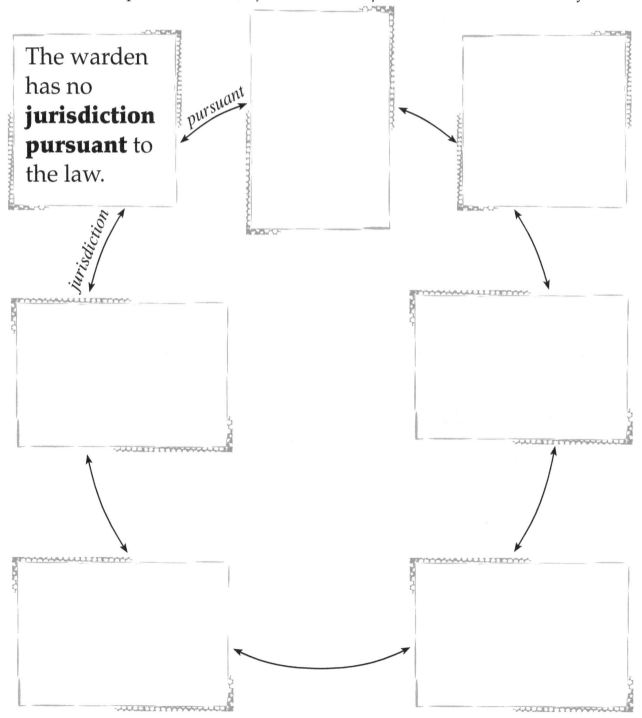

The warden has no **jurisdiction pursuant** to the law.

Analyzing the Literature

Provided below are discussion questions you can use in small groups, with the whole class, or for written assignments. Each question is given at two levels so you can choose the right question for each group of students. Activity sheets with these questions are provided (pages 58–59) if you want students to write their responses. For each question, a few key discussion points are provided for your reference.

Story Element	■ Level 1	▲ Level 2	Key Discussion Points
Plot	For what reasons does Stanley decide to go back to find the treasure?	What evidence does the book give to show why Stanley wants to go back to look for the treasure?	Stanley makes a connection between Kissin' Kate Barlow and the holes he's been digging. So, Stanley thinks the treasure may really exist.
Setting	How would you describe Big Thumb?	What connections can you make with Big Thumb now and how it was over a hundred years ago?	Big Thumb is a mountain in the middle of the desert. A hundred years ago, a lake surrounded it. There was water on the inside of the mountain. It grew onions that had a distinctive taste and smell. Shade was provided by the protruding top piece, and it was steep.
Character	Describe what you learn about Zero's life before Camp Green Lake.	In what ways are Zero and Stanley connected to one another?	Zero and his mother were homeless for a while. Zero became a ward of the state when his mother left. He stole Clyde Livingston's shoes and then threw them over the bridge. This was the pair that hit Stanley.
Character	How is Stanley's life different since he found the treasure?	Compare and contrast Stanley's life now to how it was before Camp Green Lake.	Stanley's family has become rich from his father's invention. Stanley is found innocent of the earlier crime. Zero has become a member of the family. The family no longer has to worry about being evicted from their home.

Name _____

Date _____

Analyzing the Literature

Directions: Think about the section you have just read. Read each question and state your response with textual evidence.

1. For what reasons does Stanley decide to go back to find the treasure?

_____

_____

_____

_____

2. How would you describe Big Thumb?

_____

_____

_____

_____

3. Describe what you learn about Zero's life before Camp Green Lake.

_____

_____

_____

_____

4. How is Stanley's life different since he found the treasure?

_____

_____

_____

_____

Name _____

Date _____

▲ Analyzing the Literature

Directions: Think about the section you have just read. Read each question and state your response with textual evidence.

1. What evidence does the book give to show why Stanley wants to go back to look for the treasure?

   _____

   _____

   _____

   _____

2. What connections can you make with Big Thumb now and how it was over a hundred years ago?

   _____

   _____

   _____

   _____

3. In what ways are Zero and Stanley connected to one another?

   _____

   _____

   _____

   _____

4. Compare and contrast Stanley's life now to how it was before Camp Green Lake.

   _____

   _____

   _____

Name _____

Date _____

Reader Response

Directions: Choose one of the following prompts about this section to answer. Be sure you include a topic sentence in your response, use textual evidence to support your opinion, and provide a strong conclusion that summarizes your opinion.

Writing Prompts

- **Informative/Explanatory Piece**—What are at least three unanswered questions you have about the novel? Describe why you chose each question.
- **Narrative Piece**—Write an epilogue for the novel. Include any further information that you would like to know about the characters.

_____

_____

_____

_____

_____

_____

_____

_____

_____

_____

_____

_____

_____

_____

_____

Close Reading the Literature

Directions: Closely reread the section of chapter 42 where it begins, "Two nights later, Stanley lay awake . . . ." Continue reading to the end of the chapter. Read each question and then revisit the text to find the evidence that supports your answer.

1. Use evidence from the text to describe why Stanley is happy and can't fall asleep.

   _____

   _____

   _____

2. Based on this section, what causes Stanley to think that he and Zero should try to find the buried treasure chest?

   _____

   _____

   _____

3. What text evidence helps the reader understand why Stanley no longer sees the shoes hitting him on the head as a curse, but rather destiny?

   _____

   _____

   _____

4. Use the text to describe what plan Stanley has come up with to keep them from having to return to Camp Green Lake.

   _____

   _____

   _____

Name _____

Date _____

Making Connections—Happily Ever After

Stanley's family always has bad luck. Eventually, their luck turns around. Not only does Stanley's father invent a foot-odor eliminator, but Stanley and Zero both receive large sums of money because they found the treasure. They spend their money to better themselves and their families.

Directions: If you received a million dollars, what would you do? What would you buy? Fill in the chart below with your plan and what each item might cost. Try to think of resources that would help you get the most out of your money.

Item	Expense

Total Spent: _____

Name _____

Date _____

Creating with the Story Elements

Directions: Thinking about the story elements of character, setting, and plot in a novel is very important to understanding what is happening and why. Complete **one** of the following activities about what you've read so far. Be creative and have fun!

Characters

Stanley has changed a great deal from the beginning of the story to the end. Create a Venn diagram to compare and contrast Stanley from the beginning of the story to Stanley at the end of the story. Make sure to include how he has changed physically as well as how he's changed on the inside.

Setting

Now that Camp Green Lake is set to become a Girl Scout camp, what do you imagine it will look like? Create an illustration of the new Camp Green Lake.

Plot

Stanley mentions that he's glad Zero stole those sneakers and that they landed on his head. How would the plot have changed if Stanley and Zero never became friends? Outline a new story detailing how the plot would have changed, where the story would have gone, and how it would have ended.

Name _____

Date _____

Post-Reading Theme Thoughts

Directions: Read each of the statements in the first column. Choose a main character from *Holes*. Think about that character's point of view. From that character's perspective, decide if the character would agree or disagree with the statements. Record the character's opinion by marking an *X* in Agree or Disagree for each statement. Explain your choices in the third column using text evidence.

Character I Chose: _____

Statement	Agree	Disagree	Explain Your Answer
Fate controls what will happen in your life.			
The most important people in life are your friends.			
People sometimes take advantage of the power that is given to them.			
The lives of your ancestors affect you today.			

64   #40207—*Instructional Guide: Holes*

© *Shell Education*

Name _____

Date _____

Culminating Activity: Isn't It Ironic?

Directions: Irony is spoken or written words that mean the opposite of their usual meaning. You can think of it as a contradiction. An example of irony in *Holes* is that Camp Green Lake is not a camp and there is no lake. Using complete sentences, describe in detail what is ironic about each statement.

Ironic Statement	How Is It Ironic?
Mr. Sir says that after Stanley finishes digging, "The rest of the day is yours."	
Clyde Livingston's nickname was "Sweet Feet."	
Stanley's father invents a cure for foot odor the day after Stanley carries Zero up the mountain.	
Stanley's father's invention smells like peaches.	

Name _____

Date _____

Culminating Activity:
Isn't It Ironic *(cont.)*

Directions: When you have a good understanding of what irony is and how it plays an important role in this book, select one of the culminating projects below to complete.

- It is ironic that Mr. Sir says, "You're not in the Girl Scouts anymore" because at the end of the book, the camp becomes a camp for Girl Scouts. Create a model showing what Camp Green Lake looks like while Stanley and the other campers are there compared to what you imagine it to look like when it is a Girl Scout camp.

- Create a poster for Sploosh (the foot odor spray invented by Stanley's father) with Clyde "Sweet Feet" Livingston as the spokesman.

- If Camp Green Lake were to have its own restaurant what would be on the menu? Create a menu using items that represent ironic symbols in the story (for example, Camp Green Lake water or Girl Scout cookies).

Name _____

Date _____

Comprehension Assessment

Directions: Circle the best response to each question.

1. What is the meaning of the word *delirious* as it is used in the book?

   A. when you become uncontrollably excited

   B. when you become sad and depressed

   C. when you become incoherent or hallucinate

   D. when you struggle to see anything at all

2. Which detail from the book best supports your answer to question 1?

   E. Stanley's great-grandfather is delirious after being stranded on Big Thumb.

   F. Kate Barlow is delirious after realizing she likes Sam.

   G. Stanley is delirious when he takes the truck and goes to find Zero.

   H. The onions that Stanley and Zero eat make them delirious.

3. Use this Venn diagram to compare and contrast Stanley's character from the beginning of the book to his character at the end of the book. Be sure to use not only physical characteristics but personality as well.

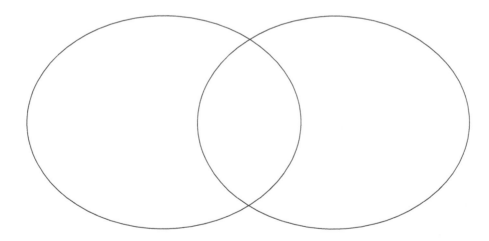

4. Choose **two** supporting details from those below to add to the graphic organizer above.

   A. He has courage to stand up for what is right.

   B. He tells the truth about Camp Green Lake.

   C. He steals a sack of sunflower seeds.

   D. He never gives up.

Comprehension Assessment (cont.)

5. What type of conflict is occurring in the following quotation: "Stanley was not a bad kid. He was innocent of the crime for which he was convicted."

   E. Person vs. Person

   F. Person vs. Society

   G. Person vs. Nature

   H. Person vs. Self

6. The lizards do not bite Stanley and Zero because . . .

   A. They did not move.

   B. They had been eating onions, and the lizards don't like onion blood.

   C. They bathed in the onion water up on Big Thumb.

   D. They were able to outrun the lizards.

7. What is the purpose of this quotation from the book: "A short while later both boys fell asleep. Behind them the sky had turned dark, and for the first time in over a hundred years, a drop of rain fell into the empty lake."

   _____

   _____

   _____

   _____

   _____

8. Which other quotation from the story serves a similar purpose?

   E. "Stanley's mother insists that there never was a curse."

   F. "You're going to be digging for a long time. You and your children, and their children, can dig for the next hundred years and never find it."

   G. "Stanley's father invented his cure for foot odor the day after the great-great-grandson of Elya Yelnats carried the great-great-great-grandson of Madame Zeroni up the mountain."

   H. "One hundred and ten years ago, Green Lake was the largest lake in Texas."

Name _____

Date _____

Response to Literature: Which Storyline Is Better?

Overview: There are three storylines that run throughout *Holes*. The first story tells of how Stanley's family has been cursed starting with his great-great grandfather. Another story tells the tale of Kissin' Kate Barlow as a feared outlaw seeking revenge. Finally, there is the most prominent story of Stanley's experiences at Camp Green Lake. Louis Sachar has done a remarkable job at keeping all three storylines separate and then intertwining them at the right time.

Directions: Select one of the storylines below and write a persuasive argument based on your opinion regarding which one you prefer.

- Stanley Yelnat's bad luck
- Kissin' Kate Barlow tale
- Stanley at Camp Green Lake

Your essay response to one of the storylines should follow these guidelines:

- State which storyline you are responding to.
- Give at least three text-based reasons for your opinion.
- Write at least 500 words.
- Use at least four pieces of evidence from the book to support your opinion on the storyline.
- Provide a conclusion that summarizes your thoughts on the storyline you chose to write about.

    Final essays are due on _____.

Name _____

Date _____

Response to Literature Rubric

Directions: Use this rubric to evaluate student responses.

	Exceptional Writing	Quality Writing	Developing Writing
Focus and Organization	☐ States a clear opinion and elaborates well. Engages the reader from hook through the middle to the conclusion. Demonstrates clear understanding of the intended audience and purpose of the piece.	☐ Provides a clear and consistent opinion. Maintains a clear perspective and supports it through elaborating details. Makes the opinion clear in the opening hook and summarizes well in the conclusion.	☐ Provides an inconsistent point of view. Does not support the topic adequately or misses pertinent information. Provides lack of clarity in the beginning, middle, and conclusion.
Text Evidence	☐ Provides comprehensive and accurate support. Includes relevant and worthwhile text references.	☐ Provides limited support. Provides few supporting text references.	☐ Provides very limited support for the text. Provides no supporting text references.
Written Expression	☐ Uses descriptive and precise language with clarity and intention. Maintains a consistent voice and uses an appropriate tone that supports meaning. Uses multiple sentence types and transitions well between ideas.	☐ Uses a broad vocabulary. Maintains a consistent voice and supports a tone and feelings through language. Varies sentence length and word choices.	☐ Uses a limited and unvaried vocabulary. Provides an inconsistent or weak voice and tone. Provides little to no variation in sentence type and length.
Language Conventions	☐ Capitalizes, punctuates, and spells accurately. Demonstrates complete thoughts within sentences, with accurate subject-verb agreement. Uses paragraphs appropriately and with clear purpose.	☐ Capitalizes, punctuates, and spells accurately. Demonstrates complete thoughts within sentences and appropriate grammar. Paragraphs are properly divided and supported.	☐ Incorrectly capitalizes, punctuates, and spells. Uses fragmented or run-on sentences. Utilizes poor grammar overall. Paragraphs are poorly divided and developed.

The responses provided here are just examples of what the students may answer. Many accurate responses are possible for the questions throughout this unit.

During-Reading Vocabulary Activity— Section 1: Chapters 1–7 (page 16)

1. Stanley and his family have **persevered** through many years of bad luck to keep trying to find success.

2. Camp Green Lake is **desolate** and barren. The lake is empty, and there aren't many living things. It doesn't rain.

Close Reading the Literature—Section 1: Chapters 1–7 (page 21)

1. The judge states that discipline could help Stanley's character.

2. The Stanley Yelnats in court comes across as a criminal who stole shoes that were going to be auctioned off. He seems like someone who needs some discipline.

3. Stanley is looking forward to going to Camp Green Lake because he has never been to a camp before.

4. People will have a hard time trusting someone who is convicted of stealing shoes. Stanley will continue to feel sorry for himself.

During-Reading Vocabulary Activity— Section 2: Chapters 8–17 (page 26)

1. Stanley has seen the **engraved** initials K.B. before. They are digging to find more treasures related to the tube.

2. X-Ray won't talk to Stanley about the tube found while in the cabin because he is **paranoid**. X-Ray tells Stanley that they are being watched in their bunks, in the wreck room, and in the showers.

Close Reading the Literature—Section 2: Chapters 8–17 (page 31)

1. Stanley wants to keep the tube for himself. He finds it and thinks he deserves some time off.

2. He keeps turning the tube over in his hands, and he tells Zigzag it's nothing when he asks what Stanley has.

3. He is becoming stronger, he has lost some weight, and his hands are calloused.

4. He has seen the design somewhere before or at least seen something that looks like it.

Close Reading the Literature—Section 3: Chapters 18–28 (page 41)

1. When Kate goes to the sheriff, he is drunk and tries to get her to kiss him. He will not help her at all.

2. The people of Green Lake do not like the idea of an African American kissing a white woman. They have stated that it is against the law, and Sam will be hanged. When Sam and Kate try to escape town, Sam is shot and Kate is taken away.

3. They try to escape on Mary Lou first, but they won't have enough time. So they take off in Sam's boat only to be caught by Trout Walker.

4. Kate becomes an outlaw, one who robs people and banks. She leaves a trail of death and destruction as she goes.

During-Reading Vocabulary Activity— Section 4: Chapters 29–39 (page 46)

1. Stanley **feebly** pushes Zigzag, and then Zigzag starts to punch Stanley. Stanley is then attacked by all the other boys, except Zero.

2. The **protruding** boat provides shelter for Zero who has been seeking refuge. It has the name *Mary Lou*, which is the same name as Sam's donkey.

Close Reading the Literature—Section 4: Chapters 29–39 (page 51)

1. He will never again dig another hole at Camp Green Lake for the warden.

2. Once he hits Mr. Pendanski, he starts to walk backward away from the scene and takes off into the desert by himself. Nobody goes after him.

3. Zero helps get the other boys off of Stanley. Mr. Sir shoots his gun to get them to stop, and the warden comes. She finds out about Stanley teaching Zero to read and tells him to stop. She and Mr. Sir state that it won't do much good because Zero is so stupid.

4. Stanley cares about Zero and is worried about his well being.

Close Reading the Literature—Section 5: Chapters 40–50 (page 61)

1. Stanley likes himself now that he has been at Camp Green Lake. He is happy Zero stole those shoes and threw them over the bridge. He thinks it is destiny that they are at the camp together.

2. He believes it is destiny that he is to find the buried treasure that belonged to Kate Barlow.

3. Those shoes get him sent to Camp Green Lake. Had he not been at the camp, he would still be unhappy, cursed, and bullied. He is there for a reason.

4. They will go and find the buried treasure and use that money to be fugitives for the rest of their lives.

Comprehension Assessment (pages 67–68)

1. C. when you become incoherent or hallucinate

2. E. Stanley's great-grandfather is delirious after being stranded on Big Thumb.

3. Examples of descriptors that may be included in the Venn diagram:
- Old Stanley: hard on himself, bad luck, heavy, poor
- Middle: caring, compassionate, hard working
- New Stanley: good luck, thin, rich

4. A. He has courage to stand up for what is right. D. He never gives up.

5. F. Person vs. Society

6. B. they had been eating onions, and the lizards don't like onion blood.

7. The purpose of that sentence is to let the reader know that the curse has now been broken and rain will once again fall on Camp Green Lake.

8. G. "Stanley's father invented his cure for foot odor the day after the great-great-grandson of Elya Yelnats carried the great-great-great-grandson of Madame Zeroni up the mountain."